Pro Wrestling's Greatest Tag Teams

Matt Hunter

Chelsea House Publishers
Philadelphia

Produced by Choptank Syndicate, Inc.

Editor and Picture Researcher: Mary Hull
Design and Production: Lisa Hochstein

CHELSEA HOUSE PUBLISHERS

Editor in Chief: Stephen Reginald
Production Manager: Pamela Loos
Art Director: Sara Davis
Director of Photography: Judy L. Hasday
Managing Editor: James D. Gallagher
Senior Production Editor: J. Christopher Higgins
Project Editor: Anne Hill
Cover Illustrator: Keith Trego

Cover Photos: Jeff Eisenberg Sports Photography

The Chelsea House World Wide Web site
address is http://www.chelseahouse.com

First Printing

1 3 5 7 9 8 6 4 2

Library of Congress Cataloging-in-Publication Data

Hunter, Matt
        Pro wrestling's greatest tag teams / by Matt Hunter
            p.   cm.— (Pro wrestling legends)
        Includes bibliographical references and index.
        Summary: Surveys the history of tag team wrestling and profiles some notable
    participants in this sport.
        ISBN 0-7910-5835-2 — ISBN 0-7910-5836-0 (pbk.)
        1. Wrestlers—Biography—Juvenile literature. 2. Wrestling—Juvenile literature.
    [1. Wrestling—History. 2. Wrestlers.] I. Title. II. Series.

    GV1196.A1 H85 2000
    796.812'092'273—dc21
    [B]
                                                                    00-021866

Contents

1 TWO MEN OF ONE MIND

I t can be argued that wrestling has been around for as long as there have been human beings. Consider two prehistoric cavemen grappling over the biggest piece of food or the shiniest rock. Their battle was not so far removed from the one-on-one wrestling matches of today.

The trappings of the sport have changed significantly, with sky-high production values, entrance music, and each personality more outrageous than the next. Once all that packaging and marketing is set aside, however, the basic elements of the sport remain the same as they have for thousands of years: two individuals engaged in a physical battle of wits and stamina.

Formalized tag team wrestling, on the other hand, is only about 100 years old. According to the 1999 edition of the *Pro Wrestling Illustrated Wrestling Almanac and Book of Facts*, tag team wrestling was introduced in 1901 by promoters in San Francisco, California, "as a way of improving the sport's entertainment value."

Tag team wrestling didn't spread beyond the San Francisco region until about 30 years later, when promoters around the country began experimenting with the four-man format. In October 1937, the first "Texas tornado" tag team match—a bout in which all four men are in the ring at the

Hawk and Animal of the Road Warriors, also known as Legion of Doom, pose with their legendary manager, Paul Ellering.

7

Many ancient civilizations enjoyed the sport of wrestling. This Etruscan tomb painting of two male wrestlers dates to 530 B.C.

same time—took place in Houston, Texas. The match saw Milo Steinborn and Whiskers Savage battle Tiger Daula and Fazul Mohammed; the knowledge of which team won the contest is lost in the haze of pro wrestling history.

Not lost in the haze is the effect that tag team wrestling sometimes had on crowds who were used to one-on-one bouts. With the stakes raised and the number of participants in the ring doubled, mayhem was almost guaranteed to occur inside the ropes and, on occasion, in the crowd.

On April 15, 1959, Verne Gagne and Hans Schmidt joined forces to battle Boris and Nikolai Volkoff at an arena in Milwaukee, Wisconsin. There wasn't a particularly large crowd on hand—only about 3,500 fans. They were an energetic crowd, however, and a small riot was set off by the tag team match. The carnage was enough that the arena banned any pro wrestling bouts from taking place there for nearly a year.

Through the 1950s, tag team wrestling made the transition from a special attraction to a more integrated part of the sport as a whole. Championships were created, won, and defended, and by the early 1960s, most major wrestling promotions boasted tag team champions who were viewed with the same respect as the singles champions.

A shift in attitude began to happen among wrestlers. Rather than engaging in the occasional tag team match, more and more wrestlers were becoming tag team specialists. By the 1970s, it was almost a given that when two men formed a team, they remained a team, and wrestled almost exclusively in tag team matches. By the 1980s, it was almost unheard of for individual members of notable teams like the the Road Warriors or the Rock 'n' Roll Express to compete in solo matches. If it happened at all, it was most likely because one of the members of the team was sidelined by an injury.

To prevent the mayhem that ensued in 1959 in Milwaukee, special rules were drawn up for tag team bouts. Section five of the 1983 edition of the National Wrestling Alliance (NWA) *Official Rules Of Pro Wrestling* spelled them out:

Wrestlers wishing to participate in tag team matches may do so in accordance with the customary contractual procedures.

(a) In the event one member of a tag team is unable to wrestle or fails to make an appearance, his partner has the option of finding a substitute, forfeiting the match, or facing two opponents by himself.

(b) Only one member of a tag team is to be in the ring at any given time while the match is in progress. A five-second transition period is permitted to facilitate wrestlers on a team exchanging places in the ring.

(c) Wrestlers on the same team can exchange places in the ring only after a legal tag-out has been accomplished. This must consist of a wrestler inside the perimeter of the ring ropes using one of his hands to make physical contact with one of the hands of his partner outside the perimeter of the ring ropes, who shall be in a standing position, within arm's length of his own corner, with both feet on the mat and one arm over the top rope. A tag-out shall not be allowed if the wrestler on the outside of the ring is not appropriately positioned.

(d) The referee may, at his discretion, disallow any tag-out which he does not see or which he has reason to believe did not occur in accordance with the above stipulations.

(e) Tag teams may consist of two, three, or more men within a reasonable number, and provided their opposing teams have an equal number of participants, except in the case of "handicap" matches, wherein the numerically disadvantaged team or individual must sign an appropriate waiver of indemnity. A similar waiver must be signed in the case of "Texas tornado" matches, in which tag team procedures are in part suspended, and in "elimination" matches, in which the makeup of teams may not remain constant throughout the match.

(f) Unless otherwise contractually stipulated, a tag team event may be won (or a fall therein may be won) by defeating only one member of the opposing team.

The NWA rulebook provided promoters with a wide latitude to experiment in tag team matches. Subsection (e) above, for example, lays the groundwork for a wide variety of specialty matches, some of which remain popular: World Championship Wrestling (WCW) has an annual "War Games" competition, for example, in which teams of five battle each other.

Yet the NWA rulebook is just one of many codes of conduct in the sport. Besides, an adherence to the rules of the tag team side of the sport is only a small measure of what makes a tag team a success.

Psychology is probably the most important factor of all. The most successful teams over the years are often those tandems that have been able to blend seamlessly into one unit from a mental point of view. In effect, they are two wrestlers operating under one mind. Little or no verbal communication is necessary in order for the team to fully maximize its physical and strategic advantages. It's not unlike a football team in which each individual player has successfully been able to ignore his own personal gain for the good of the team.

Two main themes recur in the history of successful tag teams: families and managers.

On the family side, one finds teams like Red and Lou Bastien, Kerry, Kevin, David, and Mike Von Erich, Jack and Jerry Brisco, Rick and Scott Steiner, Ivan and Nikita Koloff, and Harlem Heat. Most often, a family team will consist of two brothers, though in the case of the Koloffs, Ivan was Nikita's uncle. When two athletes grow up in the same house, sharing the same parents and training sensibilities, going through good and bad times, they necessarily

*Jimmy Hart, known
as "The Mouth of the
South," managed
several successful
tag teams, including
the Nasty Boys.*

share a type of bond that non-brothers can
never understand or experience. That family
bond, when directed toward a single goal such
as a world tag team championship, can make
all the difference between success and failure.
Close brothers will be able to anticipate each
other's moves, and will drive themselves to
greater athletic heights in support of each other.

On the managerial side, one finds incredible
individuals who understand tag team wrestling
and the necessity of two men operating as one
unit. They are wrestling's equivalent of the most

savvy and successful National Football League (NFL) coaches, able to unify, motivate, and drive forward a team that is greater than the sum of its parts. Managers like Paul Ellering (the Road Warriors), Jim Cornette (the Midnight Express), Captain Lou Albano (the Samoans, the Moon-dogs, Mr. Fuji and Mr. Saito), and Jimmy Hart (the Hart Foundation, the Nasty Boys) have gone down in wrestling history as tag team wrestling experts, the great minds behind the great teams that have made tag team wrestling so exciting through the years.

On the pages that follow, you'll meet many of these great teams. Some of the greatest teams existed for a brief time, yet made a significant impact on the sport. Others existed for years, writing new chapters in the history of the sport even as they explored athletic and promotional territories the sport had never known.

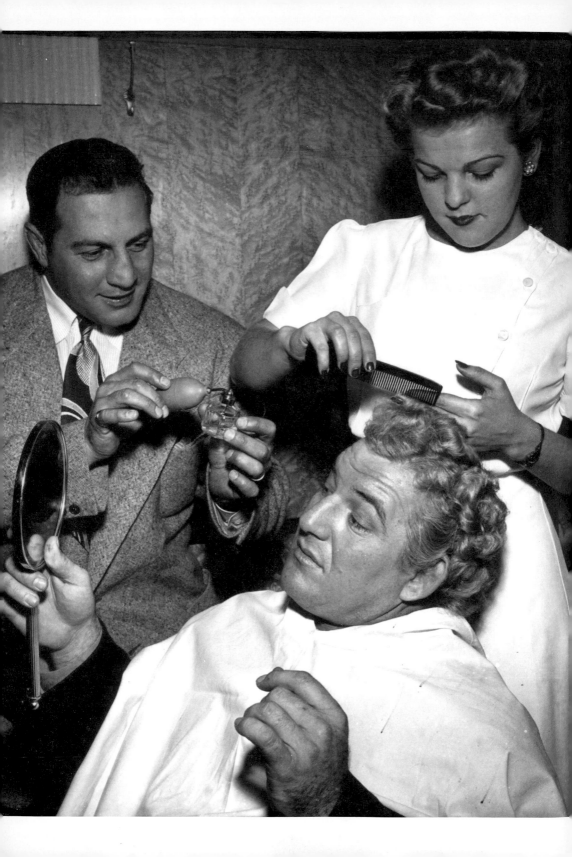

THE TEAMS OF YESTERYEAR

Professional wrestling as an organized sport can trace its lineage back to the 1700s, and the tag team side of the sport dates back to 1901. In practical terms, however, tag team wrestling really dates back to the 1950s. When World War II ended, millions of young men returned home, and some of them decided that the mat sport would become their chosen life.

The popularity of wrestling during those years was fueled by the rapid spread of a new medium: television. The TV cameras loved the mat sport, and wrestlers, in turn, grew to love the cameras. It was during this time of rapid growth that wrestling's first great superstars were born, men like "Gorgeous" George and Buddy Rogers.

It was also the time when some of the sport's first great tag teams sprang into being, tandems like Eddie and Dr. Jerry Graham, Mark Lewin and Don Curtis, Skull Murphy and Brute Bernard, Chris and John Tolos, the Fabulous Kangaroos, Dick Steinborn and Eddie Graham, the Kentuckians, the Brunettis, Antonino Rocca and Vittorio Apollo, the Medics, the Scufflin' Hillbillies, the Gallaghers, Sweet Daddy Siki and Art Thomas, and Crusher and Dick the Bruiser.

"Gorgeous" George, one of the first wrestlers ever to appear on television, was known for his preening; he always wore his blond mane perfectly curled, and he made his valet spray perfume in the ring before every match.

*Antonio Rocca
(facing camera)
gets caught in a
cradle crab hold by
wrestling champion
Lou Thesz during
a 1953 match at
Madison Square
Garden.*

THE FABULOUS KANGAROOS

Managed by "Wild" Red Berry, Roy Heffernan and
Al Costello made an inauspicious debut as the
Fabulous Kangaroos in 1957 in New York. With
"Waltzing Matilda" playing through the loud-
speakers and Roy and Al throwing boomerangs
to the crowd, a banner that said "Fabulous
Kangaroos" got tangled, and all three men fell
to the floor on the way to the ring. "We looked
just like the Three Stooges," Heffernan recalled
years later. "We never lived that down."

The Kangaroos were anything but stooges in
the ring. They were incredibly hated, in part
because of the way they used their wooden
boomerangs as foreign objects to win matches,
and in part because of the wildly verbose Berry,

who railed against the "insidious mugwumps" who stood in the way of his Kangaroos and their rightful place as champions.

They did become champions, too, capturing the U.S. tag team title three times in 1960, twice by defeating Red and Lou Bastien, and once by upending Johnny Valentine and Buddy Rogers.

One example of how hated they were occurred when they competed in a six-man tag team match in Winnipeg, Manitoba, with Stan Stasiak as their partner. The crowd began throwing chairs into the ring, so Heffernan, Costello, and Stasiak had to take cover under the ring. It didn't work. The crowd folded the chairs and began throwing them under the ring to get at the Kangaroos. Then the crowd pulled the ring apron off the ring and tried to set it on fire, to smoke the threesome out.

In later years, Heffernan was replaced by Don Kent. Whether the combination was Kent and Costello or Costello and Heffernan, the result was the same—the Kangaroos were fabulous.

THE SICILIANS

Decades after the heyday of the Sicilians back in the 1960s, Captain Lou Albano told a fascinating story about this rugged team to the historical wrestling newsletter, *Whatever Happened To...?*

"Tony Altimore and I got together as a team and we were the Sicilians," Albano recalled. "In '60 or '61, Tony and myself wrestled in Chicago with Johnny Gilbert, Johnny Kace, Billy Goelz, and big Moose Cholak. It was funny when we went out there, because we went out there with these black gloves on. We were on TV yelling 'Mafia!' We got a call at the hotel from a barber who knew us. He said in Italian, 'What are you guys doing?' I asked, 'What do you mean?' He said, "You were on TV with the black glove on, like you're signifying the Mafia. It's degrading to the Italians. You'd better get rid of the glove."

"Tony said, 'What should we do?' I said, 'We're takin' the glove off!' I didn't wanna be found floating down the Chicago River or Lake Michigan. So that was the end of that number. The glove came off and we just wore the jackets and the hats."

They also wore championship belts, having captured the U.S. tag team title in 1967. They held the belts for only two weeks, though, before being defeated by Spiros Arion and Bruno Sammartino.

While the Sicilians may have been Altimore's greatest claim to ring fame, it was just a start for Albano, who went on to tag team greatness as the "Manager of Champions" in the World Wrestling Federation (WWF), guiding 13 different duos to 17 WWF World tag team championships.

THE BASTIEN BROTHERS

Sometimes called "Wrestling's Fabulous Redheads," Lou and Red Bastien were enormously popular in the early 1960s. They held the U.S. tag team title three times in 1960 alone, defeating Eddie and Dr. Jerry Graham twice for the belts, as well as the Fabulous Kangaroos.

After wrestling throughout the east for about a year and a half, the Bastiens made their way to the Indiana and Ohio regions, where they feuded with top teams like Art Neilson and Roy Shires. Even at a time when wrestling was very regionalized, the legend of the Bastiens spread nationally. "With people recognizing us everywhere we went," Lou said in 1961, "I got to know how the President of the United States must feel."

Because of their success in the ring and with the fans, in the early 1960s the Bastiens were entertaining offers from promoters as far away as India and Australia. "I can't get over it," Lou said at the time. "Today we can write our own ticket to practically any place in the world."

That modesty, coupled with solid scientific wrestling and cooperative teamwork in the ring, helped keep the Bastiens on top of the tag team scene in the early 1960s.

CRUSHER AND DICK THE BRUISER

It wasn't very often that a tag team in the 1960s was a team for a very long time. Usually, two men would come together for a while, and if they met with success they continued wrestling as a team; if not, they split up. A team like the Fabulous Kangaroos—a genuine team that remained a team even when one of the members was replaced by another man—was still rare in the sport.

When Crusher and Dick the Bruiser got together, they were a success. Bruiser and Crusher were well named. They weren't pretty, and their ring styles were anything but sophisticated, but they were remarkably effective.

The 1960s was a glory decade for the now-defunct American Wrestling Association (AWA), and Crusher and Bruiser ruled the AWA tag team scene. They held the AWA World tag team title four times in the '60s (and once more in the '70s), defeating brutal teams like Ivan and Karol Kalmikoff, Larry Hennig and Harley

*Dick the Bruiser,
top, brawled his
way to five AWA
tag team titles with
the Crusher in the
1950s and '60s.*

Race, Mitsu Arakawa and Dr. Moto, and Verne
Gagne and Moose Evans to capture the belts.
Moreover, their success was characterized by
longevity: their title reigns in the volatile AWA of
the '60s averaged about eight months. When
they campaigned successfully for the belts in
the '70s, their reign lasted nearly a year.

Crusher teamed with other partners over
the years, winning the AWA belts with Verne
Gagne in 1965, and Billy Robinson in 1974.
Those teams, however, never met with the kind of
championship success (the Gagne reign lasted
two weeks) or public acclaim as Bruiser and
Crusher. They simply clicked as a tandem,
turned brawling into a science, and became
1960s pro wrestling legends in the process.

3   THE 1970s

I f the 1960s was an era of tag team wrestling finding itself, of individuals forming tandems to see what did and didn't work in the tag team arena, the 1970s was an era that saw a refinement of the experiments made in the '60s. Tag team wrestling was coming into its own, no longer the odd match on a card of one-on-one bouts. Fans began to follow teams in addition to individual wrestlers.

Disparate individuals still teamed, but they worked a little bit harder than before to make the team work. One couldn't find two more different wrestlers than handsome Tony Garea and massive Haystacks Calhoun, yet they held the WWF World tag team title for nearly four months in 1973. In the AWA, the unusual team of Verne Gagne and "Mad Dog" Vachon enjoyed title success for more than a year, beginning in June 1979.

As before, it was the men who operated with one way of thinking who found the greatest success in the tag team side of the sport. Brother teams like the Valiants and the Andersons proliferated. Kindred spirits like the Mongols, Ric Flair and Greg Valentine, Greg Gagne and Jim Brunzell, and the Yukon Lumberjacks found themselves atop the rankings.

Jesse "The Body" Ventura, who became governor of Minnesota in 1998, was an AWA tag team champion with Adrian Adonis in 1981.

GENE AND OLE ANDERSON

The fans voted them Tag Team of the Year in 1975 and 1977, and it's no wonder. The forerunner of the NWA World tag team title was the Mid-Atlantic tag team title, and no duo won the Mid-Atlantic tag team championship more often than the Andersons. Gene and Ole wore the belts five times in the '70s, and their success continued into the '80s, as they won the NWA World tag team title in 1981, holding it for seven months before being forced to vacate the championship due to an injury to Gene.

Known and feared as "the Minnesota Wrecking Crew," Gene and Ole were not particularly muscular or athletic, but there were rugged in the extreme. Cold, calculating brawlers, the Andersons also possessed remarkable scientific wrestling knowledge. Their modus operandi was to concentrate their attack on one limb. "A table with three legs is gonna fall right over," Ole was fond of saying. It was a style of offense that Ole would bring to the Four Horsemen in the 1980s.

THE BLACKJACKS

In the 1970s, it was hard to find a more ferocious pair of Texans than Blackjack Mulligan and Blackjack Lanza. For some fans, it was difficult to tell them apart. Both men wore black trunks, black cowboy hats, black gloves on their right hands, and had thick black handlebar mustaches. The gloves enabled both of them to better utilize their favorite move: the clawhold, which would draw blood from the foreheads of opponents caught in its viselike grip.

Under the management of Lou Albano, who wisely chose to discard his black glove as a

member of the Sicilians a decade earlier, the Blackjacks upended WWF World tag team champions "Irish" Pat Barrett and Dominic DeNucci on August 26, 1975, in Philadelphia, and wore the belts until November.

Though *The Wrestler* magazine voted the Blackjacks one of the 25 best tag teams of the past 25 years, they split up shortly after losing the WWF World tag team title. Lanza went to the AWA, where he teamed with Bobby Duncum to capture the AWA World tag team title from Bruiser and Crusher. Lanza and Duncum wore the belts for nearly a full year.

Easily identified today by the elastic bands he wears on his beard, Captain Lou Albano managed the Blackjacks to a WWF World tag team championship in 1975. He also managed the Samoans, the Honky Tonk man, and the Fabulous Moolah.

NICK BOCKWINKEL AND RAY STEVENS
Voted 1973's Tag Team of the Year, Bockwinkel and Stevens had three remarkable title runs in

the now-defunct AWA, holding the belts almost continuously from January 1972 through August 1975. Indeed, their reign atop the AWA tag team scene was interrupted just twice during this time—for seven days, by Verne Gagne and Billy Robinson, and for three months in 1974, by Robinson and Crusher.

Bockwinkel brought a sense of strategic intelligence to the ring that has seldom been witnessed in any wrestler, before or since. He was a pure scientific grappler who was cunning in his rulebreaking. Stevens, meanwhile, brought a sense of reckless brawling to the duo. His "bombs away" leap from the top rope won many matches for the team and sent many wrestlers back to the dressing room on stretchers.

In 1975, the team broke up. Bockwinkel wanted to go after the AWA World heavyweight title, which he captured four times, establishing himself as an all-time great. Stevens formed a team with Pat Patterson that captured the AWA World tag team title in 1978 and held the belts for nine months.

GREG GAGNE AND JIM BRUNZELL

Known as "the High Flyers," Gagne and Brunzell were one of the first teams in the 1970s to hint at the high-energy style that tandems like the Rock 'n' Roll Express and the Midnight Express would use with such effectiveness in the '80s.

Greg Gagne was the son of nine-time AWA World heavyweight champion Verne Gagne, while Jim Brunzell was the acknowledged master of the dropkick. Their mission in the AWA was to prove to the world that scientific excellence and fair play could triumph over rulebreaking, and for a time they succeeded.

Gagne and Brunzell won their first AWA World tag team title in July 1977, ending the year-long title reign of the Blackjacks. They held the belts for more than 14 months, but they were just getting started. Their second reign began in June 1981, when they upended AWA tag team champions Adrian Adonis and Jesse Ventura. That reign lasted two years and twelve days and helped them win the 1982 Tag Team of the Year award from the readers of *Pro Wrestling Illustrated* magazine.

THE MONGOLS

When manager Tony Angelo brought Bepo and Geto to the sport in 1970, nobody knew what to make of them. Fans couldn't believe their eyes, and opponents didn't know how to defend against their raw aggression, which often included the use of steel chains on their opponents.

The Mongols made an instant impression, obliterating Victor Rivera and Tony Marino on June 15, 1970, to capture the International tag team title, the forerunner of the WWF World tag team championship. Bepo was replaced by Bolo, another 6' 7" wrecking machine. The Mongols remained atop the East coast wrestling scene for nearly a year, and were named Tag Team of the Year for 1970.

In the most famous exchange among wrestling managers ever made, Angelo traded the Mongols and Ivan Koloff to Lou Albano for Crusher Verdu and some money. Albano certainly got the best of the deal. Not only were the Mongols tag team champions, but Koloff would go on to win the WWF World heavyweight title the following year.

Ric "Nature Boy" Flair, in pink shorts, far right, and Greg "the Hammer" Valentine not only looked alike, they also wrestled alike. In 1977, they teamed up to capture the NWA tag team championship.

In early 1971, the Mongols left the WWF as champions, taking the International tag team belts and their mastery of off-the-top-rope double-teaming with them.

THE TEXAS OUTLAWS

Any wrestling fan who knows the contributions that "American Dream" Dusty Rhodes has made to the mat sport probably can't believe that he was once a rulebreaker.

Rhodes and "Dirty" Dick Murdoch were both graduates of West Texas State University, and they were rugged and raucous rulebreakers. In 1969, the Outlaws left the Lone Star State to practice their particular brand of Texas violence in the AWA, where they remained top contenders for the World tag team championship, even though they never actually captured the belts. They did, however, establish a reputation for Texas toughness that stands to this day, and they were often compared with the rugged Bruiser and Crusher.

The Outlaws captured several regional tag team titles before they broke up in 1972, two years before Rhodes renounced rulebreaking for good.

THE VALIANTS

In the 1970s there was hardly a wrestler in the world more hated than "Handsome" Jimmy Valiant—unless you count his brother, Johnny. The Valiants wrestled a wild, anything-goes style that was as much pure energy as it was vicious rulebreaking. The Valiants were perpetual motion in the ring, confounding their opponents and enraging the fans.

Without question, 1974 was the Valiants' year: Jimmy and Johnny captured the WWF World tag team title from Tony Garea and Dean Ho on May 8, and wore the belts until May 15 of the following year. Their title reign also won them a nod as the 1974 Tag Team of the Year.

Another Valiant brother, Jerry, came along in 1979 and joined forces with Johnny to capture the WWF World tag team championship from Tony Garea and Larry Zbyszko in March 1979. They too had an impressive reign as champions, holding the belts for more than seven months. Despite their victory, fans and experts acknowledged that the combination of Jimmy and Johnny was the superior team.

4

THE 1980s

The 1980s were truly the golden age of tag team wrestling. The sport was exploding in popularity, and tag team wrestling exploded right along with it. At the epicenter of the boom were Hawk and Animal, the Road Warriors, also known as Legion of Doom. With painted faces and powerful physiques, they redefined what a successful tag team could be. But they were not alone. Tandems like the Rock 'n' Roll Express, Rick and Scott Steiner, the Hart Foundation, Demolition, the British Bulldogs, the Samoans, the Von Erichs, the Freebirds, the Megapowers, Tully Blanchard and Arn Anderson, and the Midnight Rockers, all had significant impact on the sport in the '80s.

In 1986, the first-ever Jim Crockett Sr. Memorial Cup Tag Team Tournament was held. The field consisted of 24 teams from across the country and around the world. When it was over, the Road Warriors emerged victorious with a $1 million prize. The following year, Dusty Rhodes and Nikita Koloff won the $1 million for the '87 tournament, while Sting and Lex Luger claimed the check in 1988.

Many teams shaped tag team wrestling in the 1980s. Following are nine of the best.

Female wrestling fans swooned over the good looking Rock 'n' Roll Express, Ricky Morton, right, and Robert Gibson, who were one of the most successful tag teams of the 1980s.

*Nikolai Koloff bear-
hugs his former
tag team partner
"American Dream"
Dusty Rhodes.*

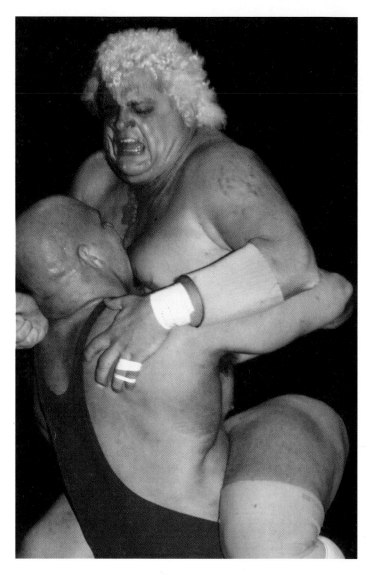

ARN ANDERSON AND TULLY BLANCHARD

Two of the founding members of Ric Flair's legendary Four Horsemen clique, Arn Anderson
and Tully Blanchard, were not particularly powerful, nor flashy. They were, however, deadly,
methodical, and intense. Those qualities, plus a
deep knowledge of the scientific side of the

sport and an eager willingness to brawl when necessary, carried them to a pair of NWA World tag team championships in 1987 and 1988.

When Blanchard and Anderson left the NWA and went to the WWF in 1988, many fans thought they had made the biggest mistake of their careers. Fans felt that the straight-ahead style of the duo now known as the Brainbusters wouldn't quite fit in with the WWF's propensity for glitz and outrageous characterizations. But Blanchard and Anderson proved the critics wrong by defeating the powerful team Demolition to capture the WWF World tag team title.

While their WWF tag team title reign lasted only three months, Blanchard and Anderson had proven themselves. Blanchard retired from the sport in 1990, and Anderson returned to the NWA, but not before the readers of *Pro Wrestling Illustrated* magazine voted them Tag Team of the Year for 1989.

THE FREEBIRDS

The Fabulous Freebirds consisted of Michael "P.S." Hayes, Terry "Bamm Bamm" Gordy, and Buddy "Jack" Roberts. Texas-tough grapplers, they embraced the deep South even as they proclaimed their love of southern Rock 'n' Roll. They took their name from the famous Lynyrd Skynyrd song "Freebird," and were among the first wrestling personalities to use rock n' roll for their entrance music.

Originally, the threesome operated as Freebirds Inc., claiming that any two of the three men could defend the National tag team title that they won in 1980 and 1981. They terrorized Georgia and Texas with their rulebreaking and

The Freebirds were a formidable tag team, and since there were three of them, their opponents never knew which pair of the Freebirds they were going to wrestle.

became involved in one of the sport's all-time most violent and long-running feuds, against the Von Erichs in Texas.

"When you're as talented as I am," Hayes said in a 1985 interview, "you understand that Rock 'n' Roll and wrestling have a lot in common. Ain't no way that one's going to take away from the other." Indeed, the Freebirds paved the way for the rock 'n' wrestling connection that came years after they first blended the two together.

THE HART FOUNDATION

The Hart Foundation—Bret "the Hitman" Hart and Jim "the Anvil" Neidhart—were hardworking mat wrestlers who came to the WWF by way of Calgary in Alberta, Canada, a proving ground for many superior scientific competitors. Hart was a consummate scientific technician, and Neidhart was a capable and determined brawler. But Jimmy Hart, also known as the "Mouth of the South," was their fast-talking, megaphone-carrying manager, and his style influenced the Foundation greatly.

Hart and Neidhart captured the WWF World tag team title from the British Bulldogs in January 1987, and maintained their hold on the belts for nine straight months.

It was Jimmy Hart's idea to team Bret with his brother-in-law, Jim. With Jimmy (no relation to Bret) leading the way with his constant interference, the Hart Foundation became one of the top tag teams in the WWF in the mid-1980s, and won a second WWF World tag team title in 1990. After that second reign was ended by the Nasty Boys in March 1991, the duo went their separate ways. Bret went on to remarkable solo success, capturing five WWF World heavyweight titles between 1992 and 1997.

THE MEGAPOWERS

The Megapowers were born on March 27, 1988, the night Randy "Macho Man" Savage captured the WWF World title in a tournament at WrestleMania IV. Helping his friend win the title he had held for four years, Hulk Hogan seemed genuinely thrilled that the Macho Man was World champion.

Savage and Hogan were an awesome duo. While they never made a concerted world tag team title run, they defeated Ted DiBiase and Andre the Giant at SummerSlam '88 in August, and led their five-man team to victory in the main event of the Survivor Series in November.

Before long, however, jealousy began to tear the team apart. Savage felt that Hogan had feelings for Elizabeth, Savage's longtime manager and wife. Hogan said that was absurd, but it didn't matter. The two men were soon at each other's throats, and their feud culminated in a WrestleMania V match on April 2, 1989, in which Hogan captured Savage's WWF World title.

THE MIDNIGHT EXPRESS

The Midnight Express consisted originally of Dennis Condrey and Bobby Eaton, and later of Eaton and Stan Lane. In both incarnations, they were managed by Jim Cornette, who interfered with a tennis racket to help his men to a pair of NWA World tag team titles.

The Condrey-Eaton version of the Express is the one that rose to fame while feuding with the Rock 'n' Roll Express. Their matches were incredible displays of high-energy teamwork. Many experts say that the Express-Express feud of 1986 produced the best tag team matches ever held. Condrey and Eaton won the belts from the Rock 'n' Rolls in February 1986, and held the title for six months.

The Lane-Eaton version of the Midnights also enjoyed success. Lane had previously wrestled in the tag team known as the Fabulous

Hawk and Animal, known as Legion of Doom or the Road Warriors, became the first team in history to win the NWA, AWA, and WWF tag team titles.

Ones, and his experience helped him and Eaton reach the semifinals of the 1987 Crockett Cup tag team tournament and capture the NWA World tag team title in September 1988 from Arn Anderson and Tully Blanchard. Their reign was cut short at about a month and a half, though, by the Road Warriors.

THE ROAD WARRIORS
The Road Warriors burst onto the NWA scene in 1983 and immediately captured the national tag team title and the collective imagination of the sport. Nobody had seen anything like Hawk and Animal before. They were powerful, dominant, energetic, and unusual. They sported

face paint and bizarre hairstyles and spawned a host of imitators.

Their accomplishments were as awesome as their power-based attack. They captured the NWA, AWA, and WWF World tag team titles— the only team in the sport's history to achieve the tag team triple crown. After winning the million-dollar prize in the first Jim Crockett Sr. Memorial Cup tag team tournament, they traveled to Japan, where they won virtually every title they wanted. From their debut year, 1983, through 1989, they were voted Tag Team of the Year by the readers of *Pro Wrestling Illustrated* four years out of seven, and finished at least second runner-up the other three years.

"We're awesome machines of destruction," Animal said in a 1985 interview. "Pure muscle without a trace of fat." "We're the best team in the history of the sport, it's that simple," added Hawk.

THE ROCK 'N' ROLL EXPRESS

Rick Morton and Robert Gibson were successful in many ways in the 1980s. Not only did they capture four NWA World tag team championships between 1985 and 1987, they also captured the hearts of millions of female fans around the world. Morton was the blond one, Gibson was the dark-haired one, and both were high-speed, acrobatic, energetic competitors with charisma to spare.

After feuding at length with Jim Cornette's Midnight Express, then losing their fourth world tag team championship to Arn Anderson and Tully Blanchard in 1987, Morton and Gibson decided to take the Express on the road. They left the NWA and competed in a wide range of regional federations, capturing local tag team titles and adding to their fan base wherever they went.

From time to time, through the late 1990s, Morton and Gibson continued to don their Rock 'n' Roll gear for an occasional match together. As Morton said in 1998: "Whenever I team with Robert and hear the cheers of our fans again, I know that Rock 'n' Roll will live forever!" Gibson added: "We can't resist putting the Express back on track every now and then."

THE STEINERS

Not since Jack and Jerry Brisco competed in the NWA in the early part of the decade had any brother duo met with such success. Initially, Rick and Scott Steiner, both natives of Detroit and excellent collegiate grapplers at the University of Michigan, had their sights set on solo careers. Rick turned pro in 1983, and Scott arrived in the pro rings three years later. It didn't take them long to realize they were better as a team than they were as singles.

With a rare combination of power and precision, and moves including the "Steinerline" clothesline and Scott's "Frankensteiner" finishing move, the Steiners quickly rose to the top of the sport, capturing their first NWA World tag team title from Jim Garvin and Michael Hayes in November 1989. Two more NWA World tag team titles followed before they jumped to the WWF in 1993, where they captured a pair of WWF World tag team championships.

Hindered by injuries over the next several years, the Steiners nevertheless continued to enjoy success. They captured a trio of WCW World tag tam titles between 1996 and 1998

Kerry Von Erich performs an abdominal stretch on Chris Adams. The Von Erich brothers were the most popular tag team wrestlers in Texas in the 1980s.

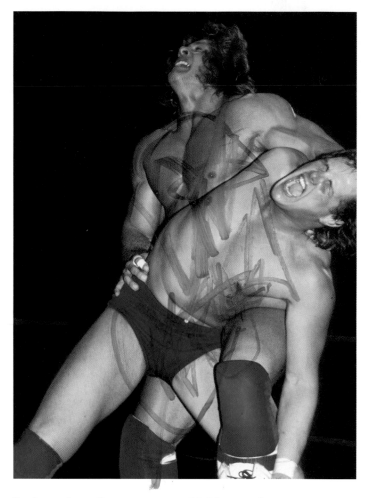

before breaking up in 1998—and reuniting a year later as rulebreakers.

THE VON ERICHS

In the early 1980s, there wasn't a regional promotion in the sport hotter than World Class Championship Wrestling in Texas. The simple reason was the Von Erich family.

The sons of '50s and '60s wrestling great Fritz Von Erich, David, Kerry, Kevin, Mike, and Chris were as staggeringly popular as any wrestling brothers could be. They were a Texas wrestling dynasty. It didn't matter which pair of Von Erichs wrestled (and usually they wrestled against the nefarious Fabulous Freebirds), the fans loved them. They didn't venture out of Texas often, but they didn't have to. They had fame and fortune. They were charismatic, exceedingly athletic, and extremely popular.

Sadly, they were also extremely troubled. David died in his sleep in 1984 while on a wrestling tour of Japan, and three other brothers committed suicide: Mike in 1987, Chris in 1991, and Kerry in 1993.

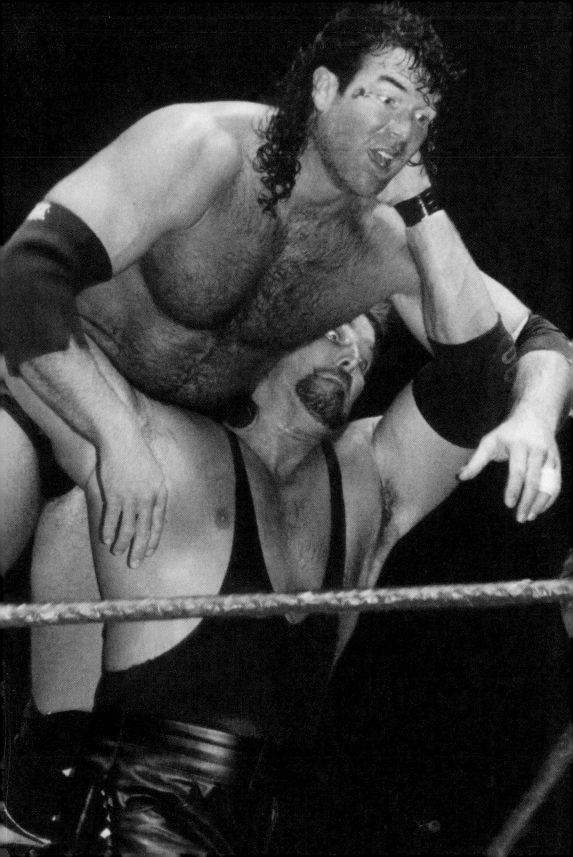

5

THE 1990s

The 1980s were a tough act to follow in tag team competition, but the sport held its own. As legendary teams like the Road Warriors and the Steiners carried their success from the '80s into the '90s, they had to make way for a new crop of teams that took tag team wrestling to new levels.

The '90s was the decade of attitude in pro wrestling, with rough attitudes and a penchant for a more extreme level of violence characterizing most of the successful teams. Harlem Heat and the Nasty Boys grew up on the mean streets, and took hard-edged attitude into the ring with them along with their skills.

Wrestling in the '90s was more volatile than ever. It was an era of, "I'm looking out for me, and you have to fend for yourself!" in the sport, an attitude that doesn't lend itself to successful partnerships between two men, and tag team wrestling declined in popularity as a result. Some pairs, however, still delighted fans.

TED DIBIASE AND IRWIN R. SCHYSTER

When wrestling historians look back at the greatest teams the sport has known, Ted DiBiase and Irwin R. Schyster will not be on the list, but they were as successful a duo as the WWF has ever known. DiBiase was known as the "Million Dollar Man,"

Scott Hall and Kevin Nash decided to attack WCW from within by forming the Outsiders, a powerful clique determined to dominate the federation.

"Million Dollar Man" Ted DiBiase, above left, delighted in paying his opponents large sums of money to do embarrassing things.

famous for belittling opponents and fans, and offering them absurd amounts of money to do absurd things such as lick his boots. Schyster was the former Mike Rotundo, a solid scientific grappler who distinguished himself on the collegiate level. Their first title reign came in February 1992, when they defeated the Legion Of Doom (also known as the Road Warriors) and lasted for five months before they were dethroned by the massive duo of Earthquake and Typhoon. They regained the title after three months, and their second reign lasted for eight months before the Steiners dethroned them. This time, they regained the belts in just two days. The Steiners rebounded quickly, too, cutting DiBiase and Schyster's reign short at just three days. For all of 1992 and most of 1993, there probably wasn't another WWF team that was more hated or more successful.

DOOM

Butch Reed and Ron Simmons were both superb singles wrestlers with football backgrounds before they took themselves to the squared circle. They both had rugged, no-nonsense wrestling styles, and they thought alike.

It was, therefore, something of a stroke of genius when manager Teddy Long put Reed and Simmons together and christened them Doom. "The only reason that Ron Simmons and Butch Reed are the number-one team today is because they're bigger, badder, and better than those other pretenders that the NWA has comin' after these belts," said Long.

Doom captured the title from the Steiners on May 19, 1990, at the Capital Combat pay-per-view card. Their reign lasted until Wrestle War on February 24, 1991, when they were upended by Jim Garvin and Michael Hayes.

If that doesn't sound particularly impressive, consider this: Doom's nine months as champions marked the longest NWA World tag team title reign since Gene and Ole Anderson captured the belts in May 1981 and kept them for 16 months.

THE DUDLEYS

Sometimes, it seemed like there were Dudleys everywhere in Extreme Championship Wrestling

One of the longest NWA tag team title reigns in history was held by Ron Simmons of Doom, who together with partner Butch Reed, is among the relatively few African Americans in pro wrestling.

(ECW)—Sign Guy Dudley, Dances With Dudley, Chubby Dudley, Spike Dudley, and Dick Dudley.

Then there's D-Von Dudley and Buh-Buh Ray Dudley, the self-proclaimed most dangerous tag team in the world. It's hard to argue with them or their success. In 1997 and 1998 alone, they captured five World tag team championships in the exceedingly violent ECW federation.

D-Von and Buh-Buh Ray won their first ECW tag team title when they defeated the Eliminators on April 13, 1997. That first title reign lasted less than a month before the Dudleys lost the belts back to the Eliminators, but they bounced right back to regain the title on June 20, 1997, again holding it less than a month. Their third championship began when they beat the Gangstas on August 17, 1997, and broke the 30-day barrier, but just barely. Their fourth title reign lasted only eight days, their fifth 38 days.

From left to right are Buh-Buh Ray Dudley, Big Dick Dudley, and D-Von Dudley, just a few of the many Dudleys who have tag team wrestled in ECW.

Despite their brief tenures as champs, the Dudleys made their mark on ECW and the sport in general, carrying tag team competition to an extreme new level of unbridled violence.

SCOTT HALL AND KEVIN NASH

Hall and Nash held the WCW World tag team title for just under a year, from October 27, 1996 (when they defeated Harlem Heat) until October 13, 1997 (when the Steiners defeated Hall and Syxx, who was substituting for the injured Nash). They bounced back from the loss to capture two more WCW World tag team titles in the first half of 1998, defeating the Steiners both times.

Known as the Outsiders, they didn't just dominate the WCW tag team scene, they dominated WCW in its entirety. When the former WWF stars entered WCW in June 1996, they did so with the express purpose of gaining complete and total control of the organization. With Hulk Hogan by their side, they formed the New World Order (NWO) and did exactly what they set out to do.

Amid all the NWO's antics, however, from power-bombing WCW executive Eric Bischoff through an interview stage, to amassing an incredible roster of wrestlers, to sneak-attacking and mass-attacking anyone they pleased, one fact seemed to get lost: Hall and Nash were as successful a team as WCW had ever seen. It shouldn't have come as any surprise. Nash, under the name Diesel, held the WWF World tag team title twice in 1994 and 1995 with Shawn Michaels as his partner. Hall had won the AWA World tag team championship with Curt Hennig in 1986.

HARLEM HEAT

Harlem Heat was to the '90s what the Road Warriors were to the '80s. The championship success of Booker T and Stevie Ray, brothers who grew up on 110th Street in the Harlem section of New York City, was nothing short of astounding. They first captured the WCW World tag team championship on December 8, 1994, and amassed no less than seven world titles in less than two years, the seventh coming to an end on October 27, 1996.

Along the way, they defeated some of the best teams WCW had ever seen, including Public Enemy, Lex Luger and Sting, the Nasty Boys, and the Steiners. They also collected a pair of Tag Team of the Year awards from the readers of *Pro Wrestling Illustrated* magazine in 1995 and 1996.

Booker T's quickness and athleticism were complemented by Stevie Ray's muscular power. They approached each match as if they were entering a street fight, and were as intimidating as any tag team in wrestling history.

In 1999, Booker T and Stevie Ray had their problems. Given their success in the past, though, it was a safe bet that they would find a way to resolve whatever issues they had between them and lead tag team wrestling into the 21st century.

THE NASTY BOYS

Jerry Sags and Brian Knobs were truly nasty boys. They grew up together on the mean streets of Allentown, Pennsylvania, and both entered the mat sport in 1985. Loud, arrogant, and aggressive, the Nasty Boys were anything but sophisticated mat technicians. Their idea of good wrestling often meant bashing a steel trash can over an opponent's head or mashing his face into one of their own sweaty armpits.

They specialized in falls-count-anywhere matches and took survival of the fittest to new

THE GREATEST TAG TEAM BOUTS EVER

6

What makes a great tag team match? The same thing that makes a great singles match: action and drama with championships and pride at stake. Sometimes, great matches develop out of great feuds. Other times, teams rise to the occasion of a pay-per-view event or an unusual match stipulation. In a few cases, a great tag team match involves competitors who wrestle with each other for only one match.

The sport has played host to hundreds of incredible tag team matches over the years, matches that provided excitement and thrills every bit the equal of the World Series or the Super Bowl. Here are some of the very best and the most significant.

AUGUST 9, 1980:
BOB BACKLUND AND PEDRO MORALES VS. THE SAMOANS

It was quite a scene as 40,671 fans were on hand in New York's Shea Stadium, home of the New York Mets, to see Bruno Sammartino battle Larry Zbyszko and Hulk Hogan battle Andre the Giant. The "Showdown At Shea Stadium" also included an important tag team bout, as WWF World tag team champions the Samoans were defending their championship

---

Davey Boy Smith led the British Bulldogs to a WWF World tag team championship victory over Greg Valentine and Brutus Beefcake at WrestleMania II in 1986.

Pedro Morales, far right, teamed with Bob Backlund to defeat the Samoans in a 1980 match for the WWF World tag team title. The match drew a record crowd to New York's Shea Stadium.

against the team of Bob Backlund and Pedro Morales. The Samoans had held the belts for four months prior to the match, but couldn't contend with the onslaught of Backlund and Morales—enormously popular grapplers who had the crowd on their side. After Backlund and Morales won the belts, though, they had to give them back because Backlund had been WWF World champion at the time and was unable to defend two belts simultaneously. The Samoans recaptured the title in a tournament a month later, and Morales went on to win the WWF Intercontinental title in December 1980.

MARCH 12, 1983:
RICK STEAMBOAT AND JAY YOUNGBLOOD VS. SERGEANT SLAUGHTER AND DON KERNODLE

Sergeant Slaughter and Don Kernodle had held the NWA World tag team title since defeating Shohei "Giant" Baba and Antonio Inoki in a tournament final in Tokyo, Japan, on September 12, 1982. As viciously hated as Slaughter and Kernodle were by the fans, Rick Steamboat and Jay Youngblood were truly beloved by the crowd. Going into this March 12 match in Greensboro, North Carolina, the challengers vowed that if they failed to win the belts, they would never wrestle together as a team again. It was unthinkable to the fans, and an incredible incentive for both teams to win. A standing-room-only crowd in the Greensboro Coliseum cheered on the challengers as they captured the belts in a violent and bloody cage match. Steamboat and Youngblood held the belts for three months, then went on to capture the championship two more times before the end of 1983.

AUGUST 25, 1984:
THE ROAD WARRIORS VS. CRUSHER AND BARON VON RASCHKE

There was excitement in the air in 1984. The Minnesota-based AWA was making a play for national prominence in response to the WWF's expansion from its base of operations in the Northeast. Two-time WWF World tag team champion Rick Martel was AWA World champion, and Crusher and Baron Von Raschke had been AWA World tag team champions since May 6, 1984. Then Hawk and Animal invaded Las Vegas for an AWA television taping, obliterated the tag team champions, and claimed their first world tag team title. They held the belts for more than a year, and went on to become the only team ever to capture world tag team titles in the AWA, NWA, and WWF.

MARCH 31, 1985:
HULK HOGAN AND MR. T VS. RODDY PIPER AND PAUL ORNDORFF

This WrestleMania I match catapulted pro wrestling into its mid-1980s wave of popularity and was especially memorable because of an unusual event that took place three days before the bout. On March 28, 1985, as part of their pre-WrestleMania publicity tour, Hulk Hogan and Mr. T appeared on the cable program *Hot Properties*, hosted by comedian Richard Belzer. Belzer asked Hogan to demonstrate a wrestling hold on him, so Hogan put Belzer in a front facelock and clamped down the hold. Suddenly, Belzer slumped forward then fell unconscious to the floor, hitting his head in the process. Hogan had unwittingly injured him, and Belzer, who ended up needing nine stitches, sued for damages. This controversial incident boosted ratings for the first WrestleMania. While not available on pay-per-view television, WrestleMania I was made available to 135 closed-circuit locations and drew an estimated viewership of 400,000 in addition to the 20,000 fans who packed a sold-out Madison Square Garden in New York City. Hogan and Mr. T seemed to be everywhere in the days before WrestleMania—they even hosted *Saturday*

Night Live—and went on to win the match when Hogan pinned Orndorff.

APRIL 7, 1986:
THE BRITISH BULLDOGS VS. GREG VALENTINE AND BRUTUS BEEFCAKE

The second WrestleMania card was the first to be broadcast via pay-per-view television, and the only WrestleMania to be held in three locations: Nassau Coliseum in Uniondale, New York, the Rosemont Horizon in Chicago, Illinois, and the Sports Arena in Los Angeles, California. The only title change on the card may have been the best match at any of the three arenas: the British Bulldogs' WWF World tag team title victory over Greg Valentine and Brutus Beefcake. Davey Boy Smith pinned Valentine at 13:03 of the classic bout, ending the eight-month reign of Valentine and Beefcake and beginning a stint atop the WWF that would last for the rest of the year. The Bulldogs wore the belts until being unseated by the Hart Foundation the following January, and the Bulldogs-Hart matches were acknowledged as some of the best the WWF had ever seen.

APRIL 18, 1986:
THE ROAD WARRIORS VS. MAGNUM T.A. AND RONNIE GARVIN

The largest cash prize in professional wrestling—one million dollars—was reserved for the winners of the annual Jim Crockett Sr. Memorial Cup tag team tournament. In 1986 the Road Warriors were hungry to get it, and set their sights on the prize. But to feast on the cash, they had to battle their way through a seven-hour, 20-match, two-session tournament

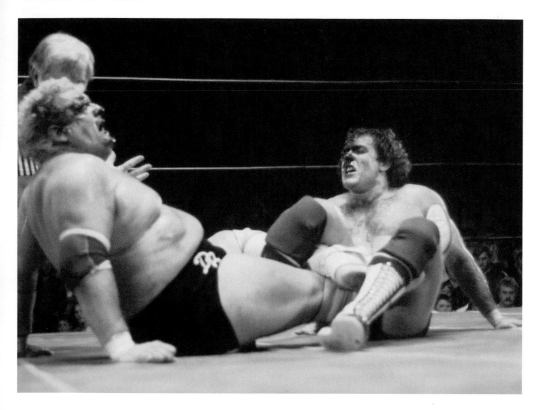

Tag team wrestler Dusty Rhodes, left, puts his opponent Tully Blanchard in the figure-four leglock.

at the Superdome in New Orleans. When it was all over, Hawk and Animal had captured the Crockett Cup and the biggest tag team tournament prize in the sport.

APRIL 11, 1987:
DUSTY RHODES AND NIKITA KOLOFF VS. TULLY BLANCHARD AND LEX LUGER

Seldom has emotion played such an important role in any match. The occasion was the final round of the second Jim Crockett Sr. Memorial Cup tag team tournament. Dusty Rhodes and Nikita Koloff were squaring off against Tully Blanchard and Lex Luger. Before the bout, Magnum T.A. walked down the aisle to the ring. That may not sound like an accomplishment, but it was astounding. Magnum had been crippled and nearly killed in an automobile accident six months earlier. Doctors said he'd never walk again. During the standing ovation accorded Magnum, fans were seen weeping in admiration for his courage. Magnum's triumph was a rare inspiration to Rhodes and Koloff, who went on to win the tournament and dedicate their victory to Magnum.

MAY 19, 1991:
THE STEINERS VS. STING AND LEX LUGER

Rick Steiner, Scott Steiner, Sting, and Lex Luger were the four most popular wrestlers in WCW in the early 1990s. The Steiners held the WCW World tag team championship. The thought of a battle between these two popular teams was almost as unthinkable as the fact that Rick and Scott would put the belts on the line against two of their best friends. When the SuperBrawl '91 pay-per-view card happened in St. Petersburg, Florida, though, there they were, in the ring and ready to place friendship aside for championship glory. What resulted was a clinic in wrestling action, with each man displaying his own particular ring expertise. Scott pinned Sting at the 11:09 mark, enabling the Steiners to retain the belts, but it was a pinfall he was reluctant to make because Nikita Koloff had interfered in the bout, smashing Sting in the face with his chain. Despite Koloff's interference, the match was voted 1991 Match of the Year by the readers of Pro Wrestling Illustrated magazine. It was the first time a tag team match had been chosen Match of the Year since the main event of the first WrestleMania six years earlier.

In a battle voted Match of the Year in 1991 by the readers of Pro Wrestling Illustrated, *brothers Rick and Scott Steiner defeated Sting and Lex Luger to retain the WCW tag team belts.*

JULY 13, 1997:
HULK HOGAN AND DENNIS RODMAN VS. THE GIANT AND LEX LUGER

Professional wrestling is a sport filled with outrageous personalities, but even so, National Basketball Association (NBA) star Dennis Rodman stands alone. His ability to score press coverage is at least as strong, if not stronger, than his ability to score points on the basketball court for the Chicago Bulls. That made him the perfect partner for "Hollywood" Hulk Hogan at WCW's Bash At The Beach pay-per-view card. The Hogan-led NWO was the perfect place for Rodman to make his pro wrestling debut. He was able to act like a punk and get

Chronology

1901   San Francisco promoters introduce tag team wrestling as a way of improving the sport's entertainment value

1937   The first "Texas tornado" tag team match is held, a bout in which all four men are in the ring simultaneously

1959   An April 15 match at the Milwaukee Arena between tag teams Verne Gagne and Hans Schmidt and Boris and Nikolai Volkoff results in a small riot

1980   The Samoans win two WWF World titles

1981   Adrian Adonis and Jesse Ventura hold the AWA World tag team title

1982   The Freebird/Von Erich feud begins on Christmas night

1983   The Road Warriors debut

1985   A tag team match between Hulk Hogan and Mr. T and Roddy Piper and Paul Orndorff headlines the first WrestleMania card on March 31

1986   On April 19, the Road Warriors win the first-ever Jim Crockett Sr. Memorial Cup tag team tournament in New Orleans, outlasting 23 other teams to capture a $1-million prize; the feud between the Rock 'n' Roll Express and the Midnight Express reaches its height

1987   Dusty Rhodes and Nikita Koloff win the second Jim Crockett Sr. Memorial Cup tag team tournament

1988   Sting and Lex Luger win the third Jim Crockett Sr. Memorial Cup tag team tournament; Hulk Hogan and Randy Savage form the Megapowers

1991   WCW starts recognizing tag team champions, and corecognition of the NWA/WCW World tag team title continues until 1993

1994   Public Enemy captures their first ECW World tag team title

1995   Harlem Heat wins three WCW World tag team titles

1997   The Outsiders, Kevin Nash and Scott Hall, invade WCW and form the NWO

1998   Scott Steiner turns against his brother Rick

1999   Rick and Scott Steiner reunite as rulebreakers

Further Reading

Alexander, Kyle. *The Story of the Wrestler They Call "Sting."* Philadelphia: Chelsea House Publishers. 2000.

Burkett, Harry. "One of the 10 Greatest Teams Ever: Can the Fabulous Ones Still Make a Run for the Gold?" *The Wrestler* (September 1999): 64–67.

Burkett, Harry. "Special Analysis: Is Tag Team Wrestling Dead?" *Pro Wrestling Illustrated* (August 1999): 64–66.

Hunter, Matt. *Superstars of Men's Pro Wrestling.* Philadelphia: Chelsea House Publishers. 1998.

Mudge, Jacqueline. *Bret Hart: The Story of the Wrestler They Call "The Hitman."* Philadelphia: Chelsea House Publishers, 2000.

Pollaro, Joseph. "Van Dam and Sabu: a Team for the Ages!" *ECW Magazine* (June 1999): 24–29.

"Rating the Wrestlers: an In-Depth Look at the Sport's Top 20 Tag Teams." *Wrestling Superstars* (Winter 1987): 22–33.

Rosenbaum, Dave. "Warning: This Team Will Self-Destruct in 15 Seconds!" *Pro Wrestling Illustrated* (July 1999): 24–27.

"The 25 Greatest Tag Teams of the Past 25 Years." *The Wrestler* (December 1991): 38–45.

Index

Photo Credits

Archive Photos: p. 60; Associated Press/Wide World Photos: pp. 14, 16, 20, 22, 25, 52; Jeff Eisenberg Sports Photography: pp. 2, 12, 28, 30, 43, 44, 45, 51, 58; David Fitzgerald: pp. 6, 32, 34, 37, 40, 56; Howard Kernats Photography: p. 46; New York Public Library: p. 8.

MATT HUNTER has spent nearly two decades writing about professional wrestling. In addition to this book on pro wrestling, the author's previously published volumes on the mat sport include *Jesse Ventura: The Story of the Wrestler They Call "The Body"*, *The Story of the Wrestler They Call "Hollywood" Hulk Hogan*, *Superstars of Pro Wrestling*, and *Wrestling Madness*. He has interviewed countless wrestlers on national television, photographed innumerable bouts from ringside, and written more magazine articles about the mat sport than he cares to calculate.